Google®:

How Larry Page & Sergey Brin Changed the Way We Search the Web

WIZARDS OF TECHNOLOGY

Amazon®: How Jeff Bezos Built the World's Largest Online Store

Disney's Pixar®: How Steve Jobs Changed Hollywood

Facebook®: How Mark Zuckerberg Connected More Than a Billion Friends

Google®: How Larry Page & Sergey Brin Changed the Way We Search the Web

Instagram®: How Kevin Systrom & Mike Krieger Changed the Way We Take and Share Photos

Netflix®: How Reed Hastings Changed the Way We Watch Movies & TV

Pinterest®: How Ben Silbermann & Evan Sharp Changed the Way We Share What We Love

Tumblr®: How David Karp Changed the Way We Blog

Twitter®: How Jack Dorsey Changed the Way We Communicate

YouTube®: How Steve Chen Changed the Way We Watch Videos

WIZARDS OF TECHNOLOGY

Google®: How Larry Page & Sergey Brin Changed the Way We Search the Web

AURELIA JACKSON

Mason Crest

Mason Crest
450 Parkway Drive, Suite D
Broomall, PA 19008
www.masoncrest.com

Printed and bound in the United States of America.

First printing
9 8 7 6 5 4 3 2 1

Series ISBN: 978-1-4222-3178-4
ISBN: 978-1-4222-3182-1
ebook ISBN: 978-1-4222-8718-7

Library of Congress Cataloging-in-Publication Data

Jackson, Aurelia.
Google(tm) : how Larry Page & Sergey Brin changed the way we search the web / Aurelia Jackson.
pages cm. — (Wizards of technology) (Distant beginnings -- Improving search engines -- Branching out — Marching forward.)
ISBN 978-1-4222-3182-1 (hardback) — ISBN 978-1-4222-3178-4 (series) — ISBN 978-1-4222-8718-7 (ebook) 1. Page, Larry, 1973—Juvenile literature. 2. Brin, Sergey, 1973—Juvenile literature. 3. Computer programmers—United States—Biography—Juvenile literature. 4. Telecommunications engineers—United States--Biography--Juvenile literature. 5. Webmasters—United States—Biography—Juvenile literature. 6. Businesspeople—United States—Biography--Juvenile literature. 7. Internet programming—United States—Biography—Juvenile literature. 8. Google—Juvenile literature. 9. Google (Firm)—Juvenile literature. 10. Web search engines—Juvenile literature. I. Title. II. Title: Google trademark. III. Title: Google.
QA76.2.A2J33 2014
006.7'6—dc23

2014012228

CONTENTS

1. Distant Beginnings	7
2. Improving Search Engines	21
3. Branching Out	33
4. Marching Forward	47
Find Out More	59
Series Glossary of Key Terms	60
Index	62
About the Author and Picture Credits	64

KEY ICONS TO LOOK FOR:

Text-Dependent Questions: These questions send the reader back to the text for more careful attention to the evidence presented there.

Words to Understand: These words with their easy-to-understand definitions will increase the reader's understanding of the text, while building vocabulary skills.

Series Glossary of Key Terms: This back-of-the book glossary contains terminology used throughout this series. Words found here increase the reader's ability to read and comprehend higher-level books and articles in this field.

Research Projects: Readers are pointed toward areas of further inquiry connected to each chapter. Suggestions are provided for projects that encourage deeper research and analysis.

Sidebars: This boxed material within the main text allows readers to build knowledge, gain insights, explore possibilities, and broaden their perspectives by weaving together additional information to provide realistic and holistic perspectives.

Words to Understand

innovator: Someone who comes up with a new and creative way of doing things.
practical: Useful; not silly.
discrimination: Unfair treatment of a group.
artificial intelligence: A computer program that pretends to act like a human in some way.
simulate: Imitate.

CHAPTER ONE

Distant Beginnings

The year 2013 was a very important one for Google because the company celebrated its fifteen-year anniversary. In just a decade and a half, Google's founders had transformed an amazing idea into an Internet reality.

The Google Search Engine first entered the world in 1998. It quickly expanded in all senses of the word. The company hired more employees, moved to a larger building, and eventually started looking into other areas of business.

Google's methods to success have never been a secret, as the company's leaders believe in being honest with the public and their employees about what goes on in the Google headquarters. When visiting an Internet page, though, it's easy to forget how much work goes

Sergey (left) and Larry (right) have changed the world with their work together. Today, Google is one of the most important companies on the planet.

Millions around the world use Google every day to search the Internet and learn more about their favorite subjects.

into it. Large warehouses with powerful computers are required to keep up with all the Google searches from people around the world—and that is only for the main Google website. Dozens of extra projects have been released under the Google name, and they are all free to use.

Google's story is a fascinating one. It begins with two men, Larry Page and Sergey Brin.

Both Larry and Sergey became interested in technology from an early age, although their childhoods were very different. They grew up in very different areas of the world. Larry Page started his life in Michigan, while Sergey Brin spent his childhood in Russia. After many years of working on their own, they found each other at Stanford University when they were much older. By that time, they were both already well on their way to changing the world.

Larry learned about computers at the University of Michigan, where his parents were computer science teachers.

LARRY PAGE

Larry Page was born in 1973, eight years after his father became one of the first people to earn a Ph.D. in computer science. Computer scientists study how a computer works and know how to tell a computer what to do. The way they do this is through special codes known as computer languages. Carl Page, Larry's father, was known as a computer expert before Larry was even born.

Gloria, Larry's mother, was also interested in computers. She and her husband taught computer science classes at Michigan State University. Their interests greatly influenced young Larry, who started playing with computers at the age of six. He wanted to learn everything he could about computers. According to Larry, the house he grew up in "was usually a mess, with computers and Popular Science magazines all over the place." Various electronics scattered around the house provided an endless playground for the tech-savvy youngster.

Larry earned quite a reputation for his use of technology while he was in grade school. "I think I was the first kid in my elementary school to turn in a word-processed document," he said in an interview. Word processors are computer programs that help people write essays or other written projects. Documents written on the computer can be easily changed. This was a huge improvement over the typewriter, which uses permanent ink.

One of the reasons Larry was so ahead of his time is because the education he received was not typical. He went to the Montessori Radmoor School in Okemos, Michigan. This school allowed students to learn at their own pace and included many different age groups in one classroom. Larry was allowed to be creative and choose what he wanted to do, which helped him develop his strengths.

Larry learned early on that the best way to understand how something works is to take it apart and examine it himself. "My brother taught me how to take things apart, and I took apart everything in the house," he

Sergey and Larry met at Stanford University, where the two were working on new ideas in information technology.

said in an interview. But Larry wasn't just interested in taking something apart. Putting a piece of equipment back together after he had taken it apart was also part of his learning experience.

Taking apart various machines sparked two more interests in Larry: invention and business. During one interview, he said, "I became really interested in technology and also then, soon after, in business, because I figured that inventing things wasn't any good; you had to get them out into the world and have people use them to have any effect. So probably from when I was twelve, I knew I was going to start a company eventually."

Larry's desire to be a computer scientist just like his parents never faded. He attended the University of Michigan after graduating from high school in 1991 and earned a bachelor's degree in computer engineering. Larry went above and beyond what was required of him by becoming the president of Eta Kappa Nu, an electrical and computer engineering honor society.

Larry's time in college was spent honing his invention and experimentation skills. In one interview, he recalls, "In college I built an inkjet printer out of Legos, because I wanted to be able to print really big images. I figured you could print really big posters really cheaply using inkjet cartridges. So I reverse-engineered the cartridge, and built all the electronics and machines to drive it."

By the time Larry graduated from college, he was a well-known ***innovator*** among his peers. However, that was not enough for Larry. He wanted to further his education, so he did so by earning a master's degree in computer science from Stanford University. Larry then entered a Ph.D. program at Stanford University shortly after completing his master's degree. It was at this point that Larry began working on his most inspiring work.

One of the requirements to earning a Ph.D.—a doctorate degree—is writing a long research essay known as a dissertation. Like all Ph.D.

While many millions of people use the Internet today, when Sergey and Larry were creating Google, the Internet was still new for most people.

Make Connections: Links

Hyperlinks, or links, are pieces of text that are used to link one webpage to another. They act as a set of directions, helping users find exactly what they are looking for when a link is clicked. Almost every webpage uses links to make navigating the web easier. When Larry Page tracked where links were used and where those links directed users, it was one of the first steps toward building a successful search engine.

students, Larry needed to pick a specific topic and then spend years learning about it before he could write his research paper. The subject he chose was the World Wide Web, and, more specifically, how web pages are searched for and found.

The Internet offers a wealth of information to people who use it, but only if the person can find a useful web page in the first place. Today, we have something known as a search engine. Search engines let users search for websites using keywords and phrases. Today some of the most popular search engines are Google, Bing, and Yahoo, but these were not around when Larry was working on his Ph.D. People had no way to easily find what they were looking for on the web.

Larry was trying to figure out exactly how pages are linked together. "I started collecting the links on the Web, because my advisor and I decided that would be a good thing to do. We didn't know exactly what I was going to do with it, but it seemed like no one was really looking at the links on the Web—which pages link to which pages," he explained in an interview.

Shortly after his research began, Larry's goal became clear. "I figured I could get a dissertation and do something fun and perhaps ***practical*** at

Sergey's life growing up in Russia was very different from Larry's American childhood.

the same time, which is really what motivated me," Larry said. He began his research by tracing links back to their source. This all happened at about the same time he met Sergey.

SERGEY BRIN

Sergey Brin was born in 1973, the same year as his future partner Larry Page. Unlike Larry, though, Sergey Brin was not born in the United States. He spent the first few years of his life in Moscow, the capital city of Russia. Both of his parents are Jewish, which made their lives in Russia very difficult because the communist party was in power at the time of Sergey's birth. Members of the Russian communist party did not treat Jewish people fairly and often took steps to keep them out of important roles in society.

Jewish people were not allowed to study certain sciences under the communist party's leadership, including physics. Many Jewish people were barred from universities altogether, and Sergey's family was no exception. "I've known for a long time that my father wasn't able to pursue the career he wanted," Sergey explained years later. Sergey's father, Michael, was forced to give up his dreams of one day becoming an astronomer. He went on to study mathematics instead and became very talented at his job, even though it was never what he truly wanted to do.

Sergey's father Michael faced constant ***discrimination*** while he was living in Russia, but after attending a mathematics conference in Poland, he realized how different his family's life could be. At the conference, he was allowed to talk with mathematicians from all over the world, and he was not treated unfairly.

"We cannot stay here anymore," he told his family after returning home from Poland. Michael insisted that his family leave Russia in pursuit of a better life.

At first, Michael's wife, Genia, did not want to leave. She wanted to raise her family in the same country where she grew up. "I was the only

Text-Dependent Questions

1. How many years has Google been in business?
2. Why did Larry like to take apart electronics when he was a child?
3. At which university did Larry Page and Sergey Brin meet?
4. Why did Sergey's parents decide to move to the United States?
5. Which two areas of study interested Sergey most?

one in the family who decided it was really important to leave," Michael said in an interview. What ultimately caused his wife to agree to leave the country was the thought of Sergey's future. She realized that he would have a better life in another country.

Sergey's parents decided to move their family to the United States of America for a few reasons, one of which being that Jewish people were treated fairly in the United States. Sergey would be able to pursue any education he wanted to there as he grew older. He would not be restricted to certain sciences like his father was.

Michael had already taught himself some basic computer programming before leaving Russia. He passed what he learned on to Sergey, who was a natural at it. Sergey tinkered around with computers throughout his childhood and even began writing simple programs of his own. "In middle school," he remembers, "I had a very good friend who I'm still in touch with, he had a Macintosh, one of the early ones, and he and I would just sit and play around and program."

The earliest programs written by Sergey and his friend were not typical for people their age. "We had little programs for ***artificial intelligence***. We'd have a program that would talk back to you. We wrote a program to ***simulate*** gravity," he recalls. Sergey learned to think outside the box as a child. That skill would prove to be very useful later in his life!

Research Project

Using the Internet, research the history of web search engines. What are the names of some of the first web search engines? Are those search engines still being used today? Why do you feel Google is so successful compared to the many other search engines out there? What makes it different?

Sergey's father also taught his son about the importance of mathematics. "I was always interested in mathematics, and I always enjoyed doing math problems," Sergey said in an interview. Michael helped Sergey improve his math skills as he grew older. Sergey's parents also made sure he did not forget Russian.

Sergey went on to study computer science and mathematics in college. He earned a bachelor's degree from the University of Maryland, but he did not stop his education there. He went to Stanford University for his graduate studies.

Larry and Sergey bumped into each other in March of 1995 during a meeting for new Ph.D. students. They didn't know that together they would soon change the world!

Words to Understand

complemented: Worked well together.
manual: Done by hand.
intimidating: Scary or frightening.
incorporated: Included as a part of something else.

CHAPTER TWO

Improving Search Engines

Larry and Sergey got along well when they first met, but they didn't start working together right away. Sergey was trying to find an interesting project to work on, however, and he got interested in what Larry was doing. "I talked to lots of research groups," he said later, "and this was the most exciting project, both because it tackled the Web, which represents human knowledge, and because I liked Larry."

According to Sergey, they "became intellectual soul-mates and close friends" because their interests ***complemented*** each other so well. While Larry was concerned with the links that connected web pages, Sergey was more interested in the data, or information, that made up each web page. Their two areas of focus turned out to be absolutely perfect for the beginnings of a search engine.

Larry and Sergey worked together on a project that focused on the connections between pieces of information on the World Wide Web.

The two Ph.D. students wrote a paper together about their research. It was named "The Anatomy of a Large-Scale Hypertextual Search Engine." The paper explained how a powerful search engine could work. It was around this point that Larry and Sergey decided to put their research into action. They started programming a search engine very much like the one they had written about in their paper.

One of the first projects Larry Page and Sergey Brin worked on together was known as BackRub. Larry predicted that about ten million documents were on the Web, and his goal was to understand how they were linked together. The task was far too large for two humans to do alone, so Larry and Sergey built a computer program that would do the work for them. This type of program is known as a crawler.

Crawlers get their name from the fact that they follow links from website to website collecting important information about each one. The World Wide Web can be compared to a real spider web; all web pages are connected in some way using strings of information, and it is the crawler's job to figure how these websites are connected to each other. This is why crawlers are sometimes referred to as web spiders. The information gathered by a crawler can be used to build or improve a search engine. Google's crawler is now known as Googlebot, and it is constantly working.

A lot of computing power is needed to keep a crawler going. Larry and Sergey did not have a lot of money or space, so they filled what little space they had with cheap computers to do their research. The amount of information they were collecting was so large that the Stanford computer network could barely stand it. Larry and Sergey knew it was only a matter of time before their project needed to move to a larger location.

GOOGLE.COM

Google was not the first search engine to exist. In fact, many other search engines were starting to pop up at the time. One of the earliest search

Yahoo! was one of the first search engines on the Internet. Later, the company would be one of Google's main competitors.

engines was known as Yahoo, and it was launched one year earlier than Google. Larry and Sergey spent countless hours looking for ways to improve the way search engines worked.

One of the most important changes they came up with was a ranking system for how websites would be displayed following a search. Larry's research began by tracing links back to their source. "I wanted to find basically, say, who links to the Stanford home page, and there's 10,000 people who link to Stanford. Then the question is, which ones do you show? So you can only show ten, and we ended up with this way of ranking links, based on the links," he said.

Larry and Sergey couldn't do ***manual*** research for every possible search, though—so they invented PageRank, a special formula named after Larry Page that is used by Google to decide how important each webpage is. One way PageRank decides which webpage is the most important is by figuring out how many other pages link to it. Sergey's skills in math and computer science helped Larry make PageRank even better.

Users who search using Google can see PageRank in action. The websites with the highest PageRank will be displayed higher on a list of search results. Google was one of the first search engines to use anything like PageRank. Users of the website felt the search engine was very effective because it was easier to find exactly what sort of websites they were looking for while using Google.

The first version of Google was hosted on Stanford's network in 1996, a full two years before Google became an official company. Google's original web address was google.standford.edu and it was a part of Stanford University's website. Google became so popular, though, that it was too much for the Stanford website to handle. The website needed to be moved to its own web address, which is also known as a web domain. Google.com was registered as a website in 1997.

By the end of 1997, Google was obviously finding its place in the World Wide Web. Larry and Sergey had to make an important decision

Google's name and logo have become instantly recognizable around the world.

Make Connections

Larry Page and Sergey Brin's search engine was not always known as Google. "When we were trying to name Google, we actually went through thousands of names," Larry explained in an interview. "We settled on googol because it sounds fun. It also means a very large number. It means one followed by a thousand zeros." Google was used instead of googol, to show that the search engine was different from the large number.

now. Would they stay at Stanford University and continue their studies—or would they leave the university and put all of their time and money into Google? They simply didn't have time for both. The choice they made forever changed the history of how we search the Web.

STARTING THE COMPANY

Larry and Sergey left Stanford behind, effectively putting their education on hold, to pursue the great idea that would become one of the most well-known search engines on the Web.

Starting a company can be ***intimidating***, especially for people who have no experience. "At the time we were really scared," Larry admitted in an interview. "There were all sorts of issues."

One of the ways Larry coped with the stress of starting a new company was by looking back to his experience as a student in leadership training. "One of the things they taught us was to not be afraid of failure, and to instead have the goal to fail a lot quickly and then eventually you'll succeed," he said later.

Confidence is what kept Larry and Sergey moving forward during the first days of their company. Google, Inc. officially began in 1998, and it

Today, Google has offices around the world, including in Beijing, China.

Larry Page's 1998 Google business card.

was already experiencing great success. "Even when we had about three employees, we had several million people who used the search engine," Larry said. It was during these days that Larry and Sergey decided what type of company Google would become.

The official motto of Google is to "make all the world's information universally accessible and useful." Therefore, the first version of the website was very simple, and it has remained so ever since Google began. There is no extra text cluttering up the home page, unlike other search engines. Google's simplicity made it very easy to use, and its popularity soared immediately after it launched to the public. In December of 1998, *PC*

Research Project

Using Google, search for Stanford University. Which five websites were listed first in the list of results? What sort of information is displayed next to these results before they are clicked? Explain how the PageRank algorithm determined which website to list first.

Magazine named Google the search engine of choice in the top 100 websites of the year.

One of Google's biggest fans was Andy Bechtolsheim, who believed in the strength of Google before it was even ***incorporated***. He invested $100,000 into the startup in hopes that it would go somewhere. Andy predicted right, and his investment was one of the reasons Google was able to initially get off the ground.

However, it can be years before any startup company makes any money. Larry and Sergey could not afford to rent an office space. All the money invested by Andy Bechtolsheim went into research and computer servers. Larry and Sergey used their friend Susan Wojcicki's garage as a home base for Google operations. Craig Silverstein, who had met Larry and Sergey while they were at Stanford, was hired as the company's first official employee.

Google quickly outgrew Susan's garage, and by 1999, the partners had rented an office in Palo Alto. The company had grown to eight employees at that time and was still growing. The company moved once more within the same year, to a larger location known as Mountain View. This new office was very close to Stanford University, where the Google project originally began.

According to Larry and Sergey, managing employees was the toughest challenge they faced with their quickly expanding company. In

Text-Dependent Questions

1. What were Larry and Sergey's individual interests and how did they complement one another in the development of the earliest version of Google?
2. What does a crawler do? How does it help a search engine index webpages?
3. What is PageRank, and how did it set Google apart from other search engines?
4. What is the official motto of Google and how have Larry and Sergey stayed true to that model over the years?
5. What was one of the greatest challenges Larry and Sergey faced while managing a growing company?

one interview, Sergey said, "Managing people, and being emotionally sensitive, and all the skills you learn in terms of communication and keeping people motivated, that has been a challenge. I have enjoyed learning that, but that's important, and a hard thing to learn."

One of the areas of business Larry and Sergey never feared was the computer aspect of the job. "If you have access to these things at a really young age, you just become used to it all, and it is natural to you," Larry stated. Larry and Sergey were experts at computers, and at first they did all of the programming themselves.

But, as the company grew, so did its needs. The next milestone in Google's life would be branching out to other areas of business.

Words to Understand

revolutionized: Changed in a major way.

CHAPTER THREE

Branching Out

Google experienced immense expansion throughout the 2000s, but one thing it never changed was its creative approach to business. Google's focus on fun was unpopular with other businesses; Larry and Sergey went directly against all the business advice they were given while they were building their company.

One of the ways Larry and Sergey ***revolutionized*** their business is by changing their logo frequently. "In the early days, we were advised we should never change our logo because we should establish our brand," Larry explained. Even though Larry and Sergey understood why they were given this advice, they did not care. "We said, well, that doesn't sound so fun. Why don't we change it every day?"

The idea of changing Google's logo each day may seem silly, but the company is known for the kind of creativity that can be seen each day in Google Doodle.

Make Connections

Google has received many awards over the years, but one of the most important was being named the "Best Company to Work For" by *Fortune* magazine in 2007. When mentioning this award, the Google history page says, "We're proud we've been able to create a company culture where employees are empowered to do cool things that matter."

The logo displayed on Google's main page changes frequently, and sometimes on a daily basis. Each new logo is known as a "Google Doodle," and it always has to do with an important event that occurred on that day. Google Doodles have been made to celebrate holidays, famous birthdays, important moments in history, the Olympics, computer games, the first day of school, and even the ice cream sundae.

Google Doodles became very popular with the users of Google, showing that Larry and Sergey made a good choice when they chose to change the logo frequently instead of keeping it the same. "Our logos, I think, really embody our culture," Larry said.

The Google culture is very different from other businesses. Employees of Google are not expected to show up to work in suits and a tie. Instead, they are encouraged to wear whatever makes them comfortable. Pets are allowed in the Google headquarters, which Larry believes "helps people work and enjoy what they are doing."

NEW BRANCHES OF GOOGLE

The Google search engine started with a good idea and a lot of research. As Google, Inc. grew larger, it looked to other areas of technology for

Larry and Sergey on the cover of *Newsweek* magazine in 2004.

Make Connections

Google is a very successful company with some very innovative ideas, but not everything it releases is as successful as its other projects. Google decided to enter the social media world in 2011 when it launched Google+, which links a Google user to other users similarly to Facebook. Unfortunately, Google+ is not as popular as Facebook, probably because it was launched long after other popular social networking sites had already become widely used.

inspiration. Larry explained the philosophy behind Google's expansion in a speech given in 2004: "Usually, as companies get bigger, they find it really hard to have small innovative projects and we had this problem too for a while."

Larry and Sergey encouraged their employees to come up with new, innovative ideas by allowing them to spend 20 percent of their time, or one day out of a work week, working on whatever side projects they wanted to. The employees of Google came up with hundreds of ideas. These ideas were so abundant that it was hard to pick which ideas the company should pursue.

One of the ways Larry narrowed down which ideas were worth their time was by listing them in order from most important to least important. "We found that if we actually sat down and ordered them that most people would actually agree what the ordering should be." Asking employees for their input helped Larry and Sergey know which projects to spend time on, and allowed employees to choose the projects that interested them most.

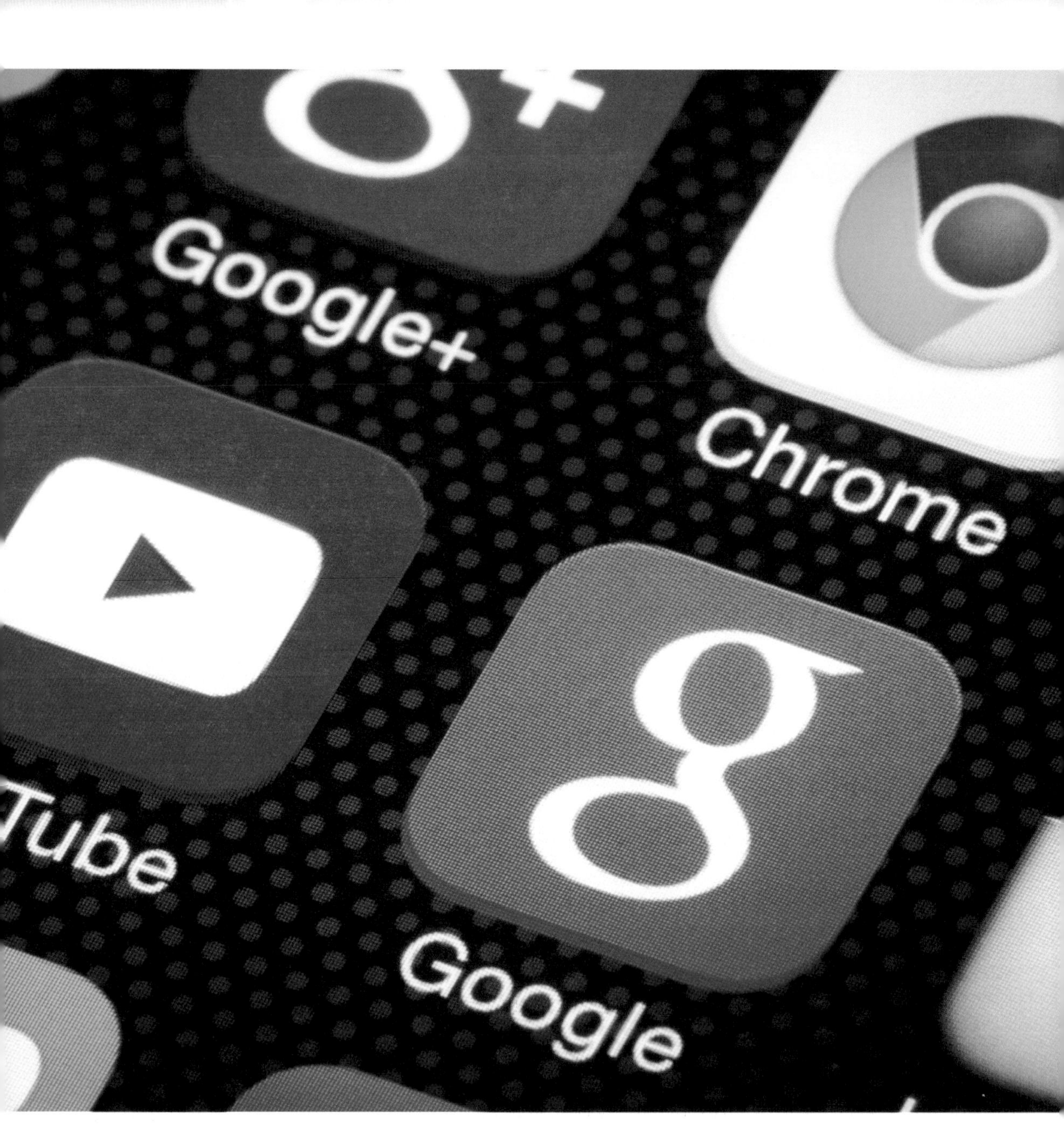

Today, Google is famous for trying new ideas and coming up with new ways to use the Internet, from Google+ to creating the Chrome Internet browser.

Gmail has become one of Google's most important and successful ideas, used by millions around the world.

This sort of thinking lead to many great projects. One of the most well-known projects is Google Mail, or Gmail, an e-mail service that was introduced in 2004. It was originally only available to Google users, but now companies and schools can use the Gmail database for all of their e-mail needs.

One of the next projects Google introduced was Google Maps in 2005, a very difficult program to make. When the program was officially launched, users could use it to find directions from one location to another, or even navigate directly to that location using a GPS device or a phone. Today, Google Maps offers up-to-date images of locations, including

Google's Street View cars can be seen driving with a special camera attached to the car's roof, taking pictures of the surrounding areas.

Google Maps has become another huge success for the company.

satellite views that are taken from space. Google employees take the ground images by driving special cars equipped with cameras down every road possible. These ground images are updated every few years. Google Earth was launched that same year, and gave users an even more in-depth look at the world from a satellite view.

In 2012, Google launched Google Drive, a way for users to "create, share, collaborate and keep your files—including videos, photos, Google Docs and PDFs—all in one place." This service is absolutely free to use, causing many users to turn to Google for all their online storage needs.

Google's AdWords allows businesses to get the word out about their companies by focusing on people searching for special keywords.

ADVERTISING

One of the ways a growing company like Google can make money is through advertising. Companies who want their information to be

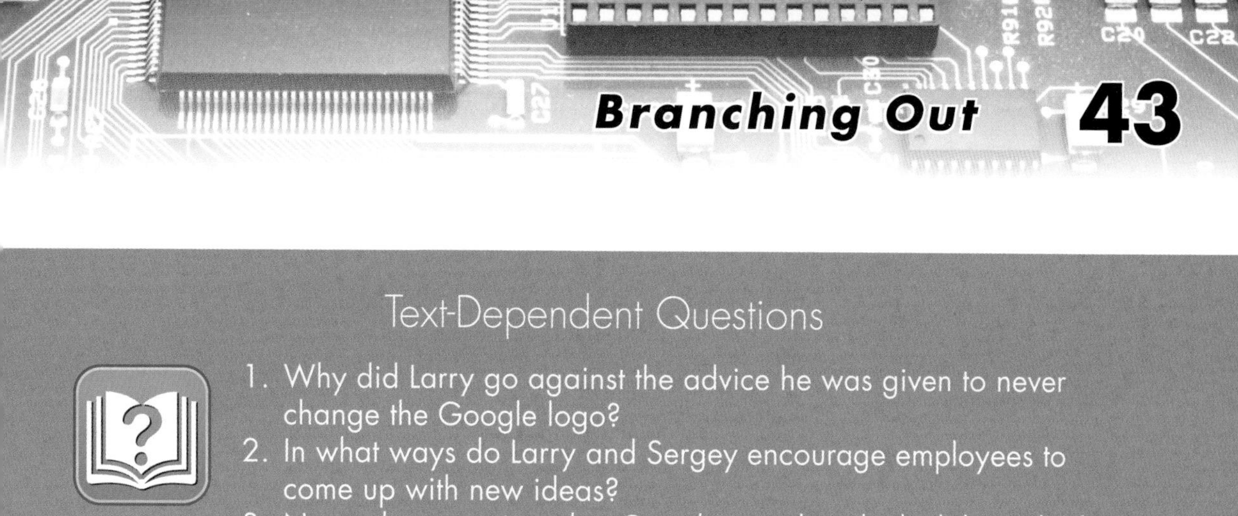

Text-Dependent Questions

1. Why did Larry go against the advice he was given to never change the Google logo?
2. In what ways do Larry and Sergey encourage employees to come up with new ideas?
3. Name three services that Google introduced which branched out from the traditional search engine.
4. Where does most of Google's profit come from?
5. What is AdWords and how did AdSense make it better?

published and shown on Google's website can pay Google to display the company's information in advertisements. These ads help even the smallest company gain attention and—hopefully!—more business.

The first version of Google advertising, known as AdWords, was released in 2000. AdWords originally began with just 350 customers, but quickly grew to be one of the best ways Google made its money. At first, AdWords only showed ads on its results page. Over time, these ads have expanded to other web pages and even to the results themselves.

Customers have plenty of options when choosing where an ad will show up. They can be displayed next to or on top of search results, in images or videos that are posted on Google's partner pages, or even on YouTube. As always, the mission for Google is to make everything fast and easy to use. "We need to make advertising across devices really simple for our customers," Larry said in an interview years after AdWords was released.

A more recent addition to Google advertising is AdSense. AdSense is a program used by Google to pick ads that it predicts will interest a particular user. According to Larry, his goal is to "make advertising

Today, advertising has become the main way Google makes money from its free-to-use products like Gmail, Google search, and Google+.

Research Project

Find out more about Google+. List its features, and then compare these to Facebook. How is Google+ different? How is it similar to Facebook? Which do you prefer and why?

useful, not just annoying." These ads are based on the content of a site. For example, a news article about a recent election might show ads about the candidates mentioned in the article.

Google Advertising has improved greatly over the years, and is now available to businesses worldwide. Businesses that use Google Ads pay for the service based on the amount of clicks their ad receives. Companies who pay more money per click are more likely to have their ad seen, but only if it is relevant to what the user may actually be interested in.

Google's successful advertising features gave the company a stable income. Based on that foundation, Larry and Sergey could continue to grow their company.

Words to Understand

executives: The people in charge of a company.
perks: Benefits to doing something.
mutation: A change to someone's DNA.

CHAPTER FOUR

Marching Forward

Through years of innovation and hard work, Google has remained one of the most successful companies around. That is no accident! Google has risen to the top for many reasons, including the way it treats employees and Larry and Sergey's ongoing interest in new ideas. Maybe the biggest reason the company is so successful is due to how much its ***executives*** look toward the future for inspiration.

The world is changing, and Google prides itself in being one step ahead in the race to develop new technology. New installments of Google's enterprise are being introduced every day, and these features are all connected when users log into their accounts. Google accounts keep track of e-mails, documents, social media profiles, calendar events, websites visited, and videos watched, among many other things.

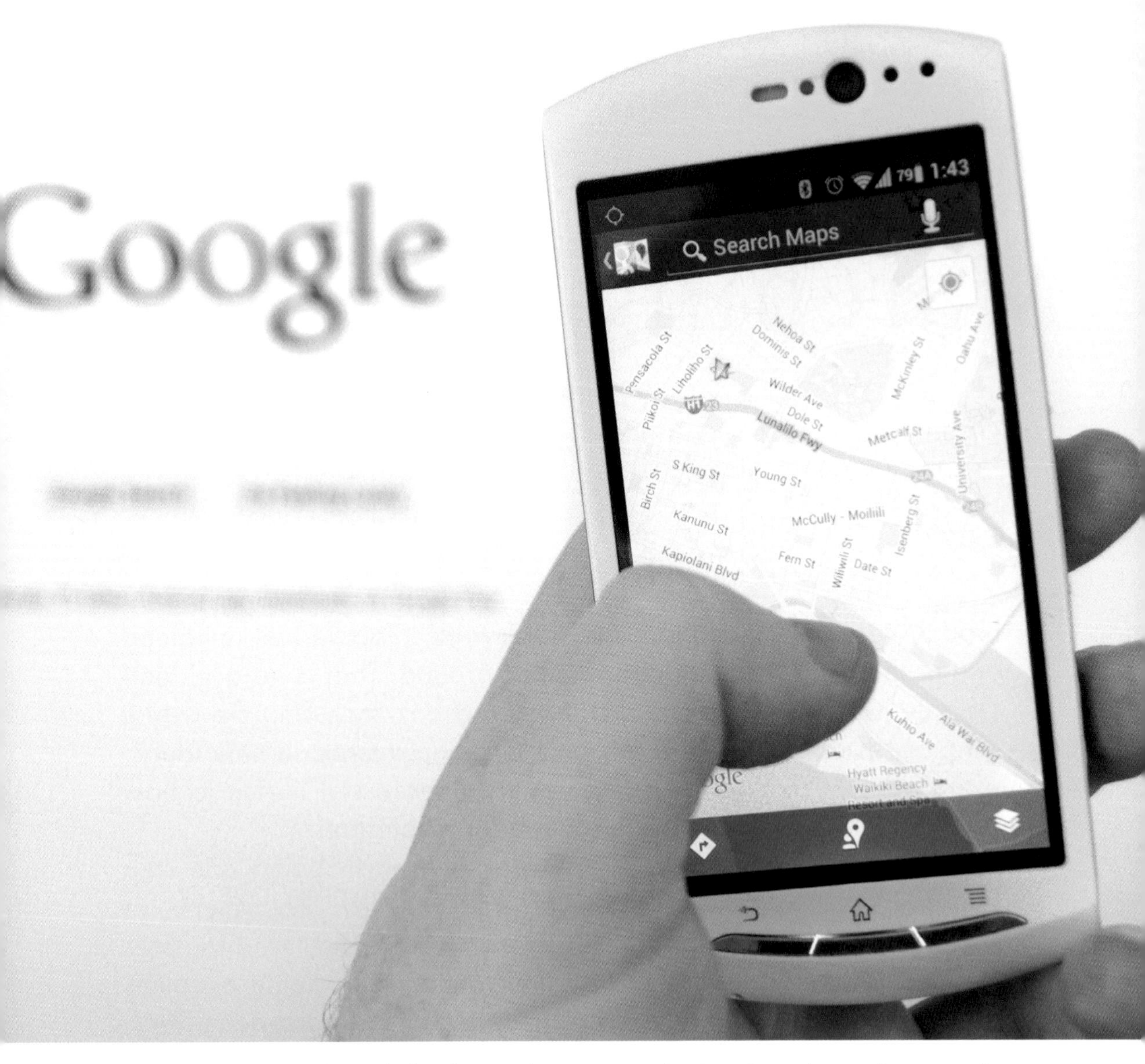

Smartphone apps have helped Google Maps and other Google products reach even greater numbers of people through iPhones and Android devices.

NEW FEATURES

Mobile devices became Google's next step in the world of technology when the Android operating system was introduced for smartphones in 2007. At the time, iPhones were Android's biggest competitor. Plenty of applications were released that set the Android system apart from other systems, including a mobile version of Google Maps that could easily help a user navigate to any destination in the developed world.

Users who view websites on Google Chrome, Google's web browser, can later view those pages on any other Chrome browser as long as they are logged in, even if they are accessing the browser from another device. For example, a user might look at a webpage on her phone and then decide to look at it on a personal computer. The webpage will show up in her history if she were logged in when viewing the website.

More recently, Google has started releasing entire computers known as Google Chromebooks. Chromebooks use an entirely new operating system similar to the Android operating system, except they are laptops and not phones.

EMPLOYEES OF GOOGLE

It's easy to see why Google has often been regarded as one of the best places to work. Larry and Sergey want their employees to be excited and enthusiastic about what they work on. "The thing that has stuck with me from when I was at Stanford is that when you're a grad student, you can work on whatever you want. And the projects that were really good got a lot of people wanting to work on them. We've taken that learning to Google," Larry said in an interview.

Google's employees feel inspired to go to work each day. "If you're changing the world," Larry said, "you're working on important things. You're excited to get up in the morning. That's the main thing. You want to be working on meaningful, impactful projects, and that's the thing there is really a shortage of in the world. I think at Google we still have that."

Google's headquarters in Mountain View, Californaia. Google works hard to make sure employees want to come to work at the stunning offices.

Make Connections: Purchased Companies

Some of Google's great ideas are thought up by engineers that work for the company directly, but others come from employees of different companies that Google invests in. A few of the companies Google has bought are Android, YouTube, Motorola, and Quickoffice. These companies vary greatly. Android is a mobile operating system, YouTube is a website used to upload and watch videos, Motorola is a company that makes mobile phones, and Quickoffice is a program that helps users create documents for free. All of them add to Google's growing enterprise.

Larry thinks it's important "that people feel that they're part of the company, and the company is like a family to them." All employees receive an abundance of ***perks*** just for working there. One well-known example is the free food provided from a kitchen that is open twenty-four hours a day, seven days a week. The tables at the cafeterias are large to encourage Google employees, known as Googlers, to talk and work with one another during their lunch breaks.

Another perk for Google employees is how accessible travel is; all Google employees can rent electric cars or bicycles for free by swiping their ID badge. Some other perks include access to free laundry rooms, gyms, doctors, nurses, and even massage therapists! All these perks and more can be found right in the building where Google employees work.

One of Google's core beliefs is being honest with its employees. Larry and Sergey talk openly to their employees about new discoveries or developments on a weekly basis. Any new program that needs to be tested is offered to Google employees first. That way, thousands of employees are testing and troubleshooting a program long before it is made available to the general public. The input from Google employees helps Google developers make the programs even better than they once were.

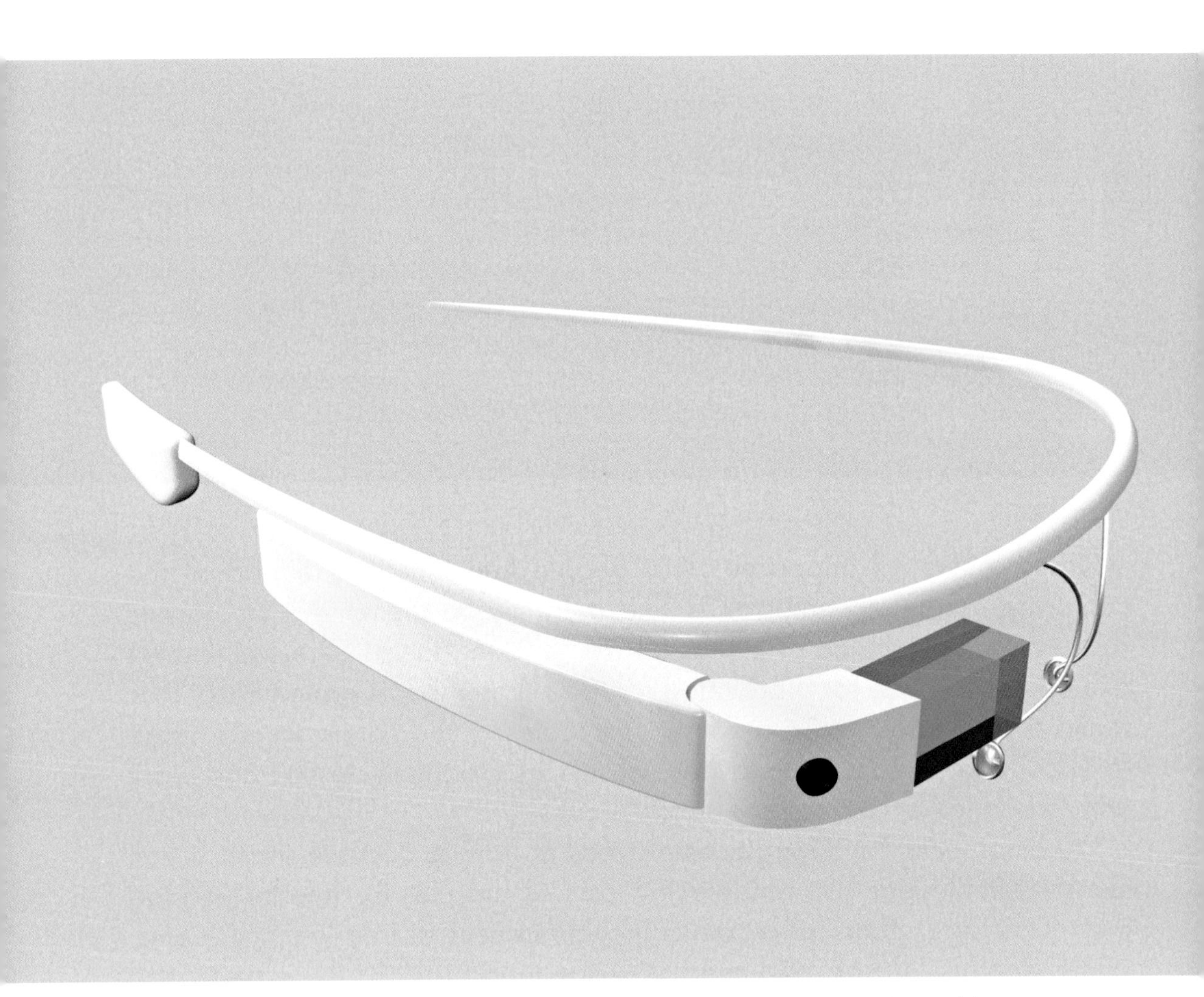

Many believe Google Glass will be Google's next great success. Wearable computers are likely to be a new trend in years to come and Google is already ahead of the competition.

GOOGLE'S FUTURE

Google has changed the way we retrieve information on the Internet in many ways. The introduction of Google Mail, or Gmail, made it easier to communicate with others. Google Documents made it possible to share documents with other people without having to send them. A user in one location could upload a video to YouTube and people could watch it across the world in a matter of minutes.

With all Google has given to the world, it is hard to imagine what it might come up with next. According to Larry Page, Google is far from finished. "I think Google is great because, basically artificial intelligence would be the ultimate version of Google. So we have the ultimate search engine that would understand everything on the Web. It would understand exactly what you wanted, and it would give you the right thing," he said.

Google is not yet as intelligent as Larry hopes, but it is well on its way to getting there. Google collects information about its users to help determine which websites to show to users first when a search is made. One of the pieces of information Google collects is location data. Knowing a user's location lets Google personalize the responses a person receives when entering a search. For example, searching for weather will bring up the weather in that person's town without that user every having to enter a zip code!

Knowing a user's location is helpful, but knowing a user's likes and dislikes is even more important to a reactive search engine. Google keeps track of all the searches a user makes and carefully caters responses to a new search based on past searches. The information Google knows about a user is also used to determine which ads that user might see. A person who searches for car dealerships might start seeing ads pop up for car dealerships on the right side of any Google searches made.

One of the ways Google has taken a step closer to artificial intelligence is by releasing Google Goggles, an application that can be downloaded on mobile devices. With Google Goggles, a user can take a picture of anything and perform a search using only that image. If the user takes a picture of a bar code, Google Goggles will return information about the product that was scanned, and offer suggestions for how that product may be bought. A picture of a famous landmark, on the other hand,

Larry Page works hard on a wide range of causes today, from charity to driverless cars!

will tell the user what the landmark is and why it is important. Google Goggles reacts intelligently to whatever it is "looking at."

To make a program like Google Goggles run, a lot of information needs to be catalogued on Google's servers, and the amount of data Google collects and stores is immense. "We have all this data. If you printed out the index, it would be seventy miles high now," Larry explained. Google is in no danger of running out of room on their servers any time soon, though. "We have enough space to store like 100 copies of the whole Web," Larry said. With enough hard work and dedication, Google may eventually become the ultimate version Larry envisions.

OTHER PASSIONS

Larry Page and Sergey Brin are best known for their involvement in Google, but they have other aspirations as well. "I want to make the world a better place," Sergey said in an interview. "I mean it in several ways. One is through Google, the company in terms of giving people access to information. I'm sure I will do other endeavors in terms of technologies and business. The second is through philanthropy."

Philanthropists donate their money and time to causes they believe in. Many wealthy businessmen are philanthropists, including Larry and Sergey. "I don't have a significant amount of wealth beyond that on paper right now, but I hope that I have the opportunity to direct resources in the right places," Sergey said. The money Google donates directly to other causes comes from Google.org, a branch of Google dedicated to helping the world.

Neither Larry nor Sergey have an interest in making more money than they already have. Both of them collect a salary of just one dollar from their company each year. "I don't think my quality of life is really going to improve that much with more money," Sergey explained. Instead of making more money, Larry and Sergey use the money they don't take out of the company to improve it even more.

Larry has many interests outside of the Google search engine, and many of them center around technology. "I have been really interested in applying technology to transportation," he said. "I don't think that has really been done. Making cars better. There are a lot of interesting systems people have designed that basically are small monorails that run along sidewalks, and that route you exactly where you want to go. Some of these things are quite practical."

Google is already well on its way to achieving Larry's dream; the first driverless cars were tested on the streets of Nevada in 2012. These cars are operated completely by a computer and radar system, and require absolutely no human input. After several of the test cars drove a collective 300,000 miles, it was announced that not a single motor vehicle accident occurred because of the computer's actions. However, one accident did occur while a human being was driving one of the cars!

These cars won't be available to the public for a while, though, since each car requires about $150,000 worth of equipment to run. In addition to this, only a select few states have approved the use of driverless cars. With this project, however, Larry and Sergey proved yet again that anything is possible with enough creativity and drive.

PERSONAL LIVES

Larry Page has suffered problems with his vocal cords throughout most of his life, and sometimes has difficulty speaking as a result. He has donated millions of dollars to the Voice Health Institute toward the research of Hashimoto's Thyroiditis, the cause of his problems.

Meanwhile, Sergey's mother was diagnosed with Parkinson's disease due to a ***mutation*** of a gene in her DNA. Doctors then discovered that Sergey has the same mutation in his genetic code, and has about a 50 percent chance of getting the disease when he is older. As a way to combat the disease and help his mother, Sergey has donated to the University of Maryland School of Medicine.

Sergey hopes to help find a cure with the money he donates. "If I felt it was guaranteed to cure Parkinson's disease, a check for a billion

Research Project

This chapter references the similarities between genetic coding and computer coding. Use the library or the Internet to find out more about the genetic mutation that affects Sergey and his mother. Explain how a mutation like this is similar to a computer bug. What strategies are scientists currently researching for treating genetic mutations?

dollars would be the easiest one I have written," he said in an interview. According to the *Economist*, "Mr. Brin regards his mutation . . . as a bug in his personal code, and thus as no different from the bugs in computer code that Google's engineers fix every day."

Both Larry and Sergey have married. Larry married Lucinda Southworth, a research scientist, in 2007 and they have two children together. Larry makes sure to find time for his friends, and still lives in the same town where his company first began in a garage. "I think I am really lucky. Being in the Bay Area, a lot of my friends have started companies that have been quite successful at different stages. So I go up to San Francisco and I hang out with my friends, and we talk about their companies and all sorts of different things," he said.

Sergey married a biotech analyst named Anne Wojcicki in 2007. They were both very interested in the Human Genome Project, a large research project that worked to sequence and map human DNA. The genome project especially interested Sergey, because it reminded him of a computer database. Sergey and Anne had two children together before separating in 2013.

Sergey continues to be grateful for the role his parents have had in his life. Without then, Sergey would never have been able to come to the

Text-Dependent Questions

1. What are some of the companies Google has invested in or funded?
2. What type of atmosphere does Larry strive for Google to have? How are the employees treated as a result?
3. What are some of the perks of being an employee of Google?
4. What are some of the causes Larry and Sergey donate to and why are they important?
5. Explain why Sergey gives money to researchers at the University School of Medicine.

United States and receive the education he did. He also wouldn't have met Larry. "I think, if anything, I feel like I have gotten a gift by being in the States rather than growing up in Russia. I know the hard times my parents went through there, and I am very thankful that I was brought to the States. I think it just makes me appreciate my life much more," he stated in an interview.

Google, Inc.—and the two men who built it—has clearly come a long way since the small search engine was first built. No matter how big Google grows to be, though, one fact will remain true: Larry and Sergey are dedicated to their original mission of making all the world's information "universally accessible and useful."

FIND OUT MORE

In Books

Brandt, Richard L. *The Google Guys: Inside the Brilliant Minds of Google Founders Larry Page and Sergey Brin*. New York: Portfolio, 2011.

Brezina, Corona. *Sergey Brin, Larry Page, Eric Schmidt, and Google*. New York: Rosen, 2013.

Levy, Steven. *In the Plex: How Google Thinks, Works, and Shapes Our Lives*. New York: Simon & Schuster, 2011.

McPherson, Stephanie Sammartino. *Sergey Brin and Larry Page: Founders of Google*. Minneapolis: Twenty First Century, 2011.

White, Casey. *Sergey Brin and Larry Page: The Founders of Google*. New York: Rosen, 2007.

On the Internet

Academy of Achievement. "Interview: Larry Page."
www.achievement.org/autodoc/printmember/pag0int-1

CNN: Fortune Exclusive: Larry Page on Google
tech.fortune.cnn.com/2012/12/11/larry-page

Google.com: Our history in depth
www.google.com/intl/en/about/company/history

Moment: The Story of Sergey Brin
www.momentmag.com/the-story-of-sergey-brin

Wired: Google Throws Open Doors to Its Top-Secret Data Center
www.wired.com/wiredenterprise/2012/10/ff-inside-google-data-center

SERIES GLOSSARY OF KEY TERMS

application: A program that runs on a computer or smartphone. People often call these "apps."

bug: A problem with how a program runs.

byte: A unit of information stored on a computer. One byte is equal to eight digits of binary code—that's eight 1s or 0s.

cloud: Data and apps that are stored on the Internet instead of on your own computer or smartphone are said to be "in the cloud."

data: Information stored on a computer.

debug: Find the problems with an app or program and fix them.

device: Your computer, smartphone, or other piece of technology. Devices can often access the Internet and run apps.

digital: Having to do with computers or stored on a computer.

hardware: The physical part of a computer. The hardware is made up of the parts you can see and touch.

memory: Somewhere that a computer stores information that it is using.

media: Short for multimedia, it's the entertainment or information that can be stored on a computer. Examples of media include music, videos, and e-books.

network: More than one computer or device connected together so information can be shared between them.

pixel: A dot of light or color on a digital display. A computer monitor or phone screen has lots of pixels that work together to create an image.

program: A collection of computer code that does a job.

software: Programs that run on a computer.

technology: Something that people invent to make a job easier or do something new.

INDEX

AdSense 43
advertising 42–45
AdWords 42–43
Anatomy of a Large-Scale Hypertextual Search Engine, The 23
Android 48–49, 51
applications 49, 53
artificial intelligence 6, 18, 53
astronomer 17

BackRub 23
Bechtolsheim, Andy 30
Bing 15
Brin, Sergey 9, 17–18, 23, 27, 55, 57

Carl Page 11
computer 6, 9–11, 13, 18–19, 23, 25, 30–31, 35, 49, 52, 56–57
computer science 10–11, 13, 19, 25
crawler 23, 31

dissertation 13, 15
DNA 46, 56–57
driverless car 54, 56

electronics 11, 13, 18
employee 7, 29–30, 35, 37, 41, 43, 47, 49–51, 58
Eta Kappa Nu 13

Facebook 37, 45

Google+ 37–38, 44–45
Google Ads 45
Google Doodle 34–35
Google Drive 41
Google Earth 41
Google Goggles 53, 55
Google Mail 39, 52
Google Maps 39, 41, 48–49
Google search Engine 7, 35, 55
Googlebot 23
Googlers 51
googol 27
Gmail 39, 44, 52

Hashimoto's Thyroiditis 56
Human Genome Project 57
hyperlink 15

Internet 7, 9, 14–15, 19, 24, 38, 52, 57
iPhone 48–49

Legos 13

logo 26, 33–35, 43

mathematics 17, 19
Michigan State University 11
Montessori Radmoor School 11
Moscow 17
Motorola 51
Mountain View 30, 50

Nevada 56

Page, Carl 11
Page, Larry 7, 9, 11, 15, 17–18, 21, 23, 25, 27, 29, 35, 43, 53–56
PageRank 25, 30–31
Palo Alto 30
Parkinson's disease 56
perks 46, 51, 58
philanthropy 55
Poland 17
Popular Science 11

Quickoffice 51

Russia 9, 16–18, 58
Russian communist party 17

Sergey Brin 9, 17–18, 23, 27, 55
smartphone 48–49
Southworth, Lucinda 57
Stanford University 9, 12–13, 19, 25, 27, 30

technology 9, 11–13, 35, 47, 49, 55–56

University of Maryland 19, 56

Wojcicki, Anne 30, 57
Wojcicki, Susan 30, 57
World Wide Web 15, 22–23, 25
word processor 11

Yahoo 15, 24–25
YouTube 43, 51, 53

ABOUT THE AUTHOR

Aurelia Jackson is a writer living and working in New York City. She has a passion for writing and a love of education, both of which she brings to all the work she does.

PICTURE CREDITS

Dreamstime.com:
- 6: Editor77
- 9: Anthony Brown
- 10: Snehitdesign
- 12: Joseph Mercier
- 14: Darrinhenry
- 16: Igor Sokalski
- 20: Lucian Milasan
- 22: Cybrain
- 24: Lucian Milasan
- 26: Gan Hui
- 28: Eagleflying
- 32: Lucian Milasan
- 34: 1000words
- 38: Marcel De Grijs
- 39: Daniel Draghici
- 40: Nihonjapan
- 41: Pressureua
- 42: Daniel Draghici
- 44: Sallyeva
- 46: Pressureua
- 48: James Crawford
- 50: Spvvkr
- 52: Vampy1

8: Joi Ito | Flickr.com
29: Evawen
36: Newsweek
54: Marcin Mycielski, European Parliament